Fiddle Time Runners

a second book of easy pieces for violin

Kathy and David Blackwell

Illustrations by Martin Remphry

Welcome to **Fiddle Time Runners**. You'll find:

- pieces using the finger patterns 0–12–3–4 and 0–1–2–34
- traditional tunes and pieces by well-known composers from Handel to Mozart
- original pieces in a range of styles from rag to flamenco
- duets, with parts of equal difficulty
- play-along tracks and backing tracks (accompaniment only) available to download from **www.oup.com/ftrunners3e** or to stream on major streaming platforms
- practice tracks recorded at a slower tempo for some pieces
- piano and violin accompaniments available separately
- a book for violin that's also compatible with *Viola Time Runners*; 33 of the 38 tunes may be played together.

OXFORD
UNIVERSITY PRESS

Great Clarendon Street, Oxford OX2 6DP, England
This collection © Oxford University Press 1998, 2003, 2005, 2013, and 2023
Unless marked otherwise, all pieces are by Kathy and David Blackwell and are
© Oxford University Press. All traditional pieces, and nos. 12, 14, and 32, are
arranged by Kathy and David Blackwell and are © Oxford University Press.
Unauthorized arrangement or photocopying of this copyright material is ILLEGAL.

Kathy and David Blackwell have asserted their right under the Copyright,
Designs and Patents Act, 1988, to be identified as the Composers of this Work.

Impression: 1

ISBN: 978-0-19-356609-5

Music and text origination by Julia Bovee
Printed in Great Britain

Contents

Section 1—New notes for second finger   3

1.   Start the show   3
2.   Banyan tree (*duet*)   4
3.   Heat haze   5
4.   Medieval tale   5
5.   Cornish May song   6
6.   Chase in the dark   6
7.   Merrily danced the Quaker's wife   7
8.   O leave your sheep (*duet*)   8
9.   Jazzy Jingle bells (J. Pierpont)   9
10. Allegretto in G (Mozart)   10
11. The Mallow fling   10
12. Noël (Daquin) (*duet*)   11
13. Finale from the 'Water Music' (Handel)   12
14. Ecossaise in G (Beethoven)   13
15. Fiddle Time rag   14
16. Busy day (*duet*)   15
17. On the go!   16
18. Yodelling song   16
19. Takin' it easy   17
20. Romani band   17
21. Ten thousand miles away (*duet*)   18
22. I got those fiddle blues   20
23. Air in G (J. C. Bach)   21
24. Prelude from 'Te Deum' (Charpentier)   21
25. That's how it goes!   22

Section 2—New notes for third finger   23

26. Hari coo coo   23
27. Summer evening   23
28. Flamenco dance   24
29. Adam in the garden   25
30. Somebody's knocking at your door   26
31. The old chariot   26
32. Air (Handel) (*duet*)   27
33. The wee cooper o' Fife   28
34. Winter song   28
35. Rory O'More (*duet*)   29
36. Trick cyclist   30
37. Aerobics!   30
38. Caribbean sunshine   31

Music Fact-Finder Page   32

New notes for 2nd finger

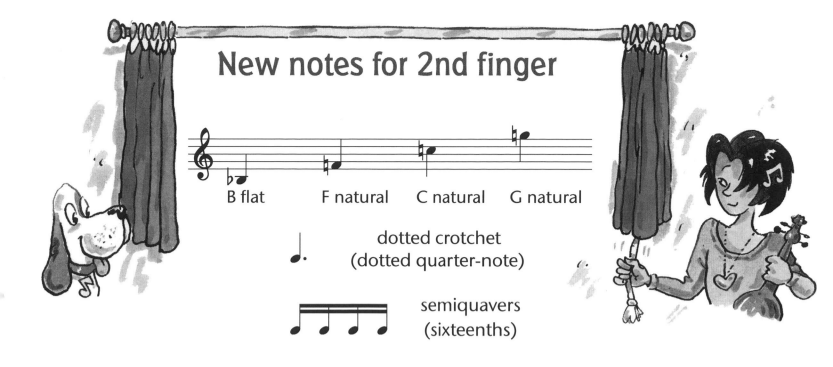

B flat   F natural   C natural   G natural

dotted crotchet
(dotted quarter-note)

semiquavers
(sixteenths)

1 Start the show

Count 4 bars

Rock tempo

KB & DB

Banyan tree

Gently

Jamaican folk tune

🎧 3 Heat haze

KB & DB

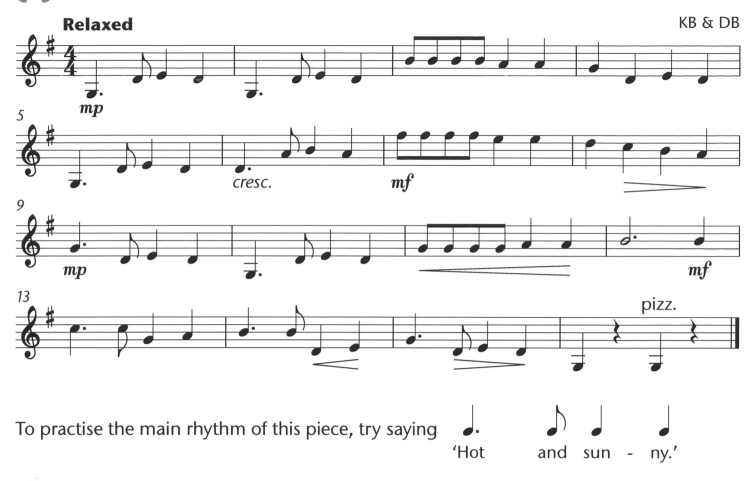

To practise the main rhythm of this piece, try saying ♩. ♪ ♩ ♩

'Hot   and sun - ny.'

🎧 4 Medieval tale

KB & DB

🎧 5 Cornish May song

Cornish folk tune

Lively

🎧 39 Practice tempo

🎧 6 Chase in the dark

Count 2 bars

KB & DB

With menace

6

Merrily danced the Quaker's wife

Scottish folk tune

O leave your sheep

French folk tune

Jazzy Jingle bells

Count 8 bars

Christmassy

J. Pierpont

🎧 10 Allegretto in G

Allegretto

Mozart

🎧 11 The Mallow fling

Count 2 bars

Irish folk tune

Lively

🎧 40 Practice tempo

12 Noël

Daquin

Allegretto

11

Finale from the 'Water Music'

Handel

Moderato

Ecossaise in G

Allegro

Beethoven

🎧 15 Fiddle Time rag

Count 4 bars

KB & DB

14

🎧 16 Busy day

Busily

KB & DB

15

17 On the go!

Count 4 bars

KB & DB

Lively

mf

cresc.

10

f

mp

15

cresc.

20

f

mf

cresc.

26

pizz.

f

18 Yodelling song

German folk tune

With a strong beat

f

mf

6

mp

11

mf

18

cresc.

f

🎧 19 Takin' it easy

Count 4 bars

Laid-back tempo

KB & DB

🎧 20 Romani band

KB & DB

Fiery!

🎧 41 Practice tempo

🎧 21 Ten thousand miles away

With a good swing

Sea shanty

D.C. al Fine

22 I got those fiddle blues

KB & DB

20

🎧23 Air in G

Andante

J. C. Bach

mf

mp

mf cresc.   *f*

🎧24 Prelude from 'Te Deum'

Maestoso

Charpentier

f

mp

cresc.   *f*

ff

rit.

🎧 25 That's how it goes!

With energy

KB & DB

Luckily, this piece is not as hard as it looks!

🎧 42 Practice tempo

New notes for 3rd finger

C sharp   G sharp   D sharp

🎧 26 Hari coo coo

Count 2 bars

Gently

Indian lullaby

rit. (2nd time)   Fine

D.𝄋 al Fine

🎧 27 Summer evening

Flowing

KB & DB

29 Adam in the garden

Relaxed tempo

Jamaican folk tune

30 Somebody's knocking at your door

Spiritual

31 The old chariot

Sea shanty

32 Air

Handel

Allegro

27

33 The wee cooper o' Fife

Scottish folk tune

Gently

mp

34 Winter song

KB & DB

Wistfully

mp

cresc.

mf

rit. (2nd time)

mp

p

Rory O'More

Lively

Traditional Irish Jig

🎧 36 Trick cyclist

With energy

KB & DB

🎧 43 Practice tempo

🎧 37 Aerobics!

KB & DB

Music Fact-Finder Page

Here are some of the words and signs you will find in some of your pieces!

How to play it

pizzicato or pizz. = pluck

arco = with the bow

⊓ = down bow

V = up bow

> = accent

𝅘𝅥 = tremolo

Don't get lost!

‖: :‖ = repeat marks

1. 2. = first and second time bars

D.C. al Fine = repeat from the beginning and stop at **Fine**

D.%. al Fine = repeat from the sign % and stop at **Fine**

rit. or **rall.** = gradually getting slower

a tempo = back to the first speed

⌒ = pause

Volume control

p (*piano*) = quiet

mp (*mezzo-piano*) = moderately quiet

mf (*mezzo-forte*) = moderately loud

f (*forte*) = loud

ff (*fortissimo*) = very loud

⸻ or *crescendo* (*cresc.*) = getting gradually louder

⸻ or *diminuendo* (*dim.*) = getting gradually quieter

Italian phrase-book

Allegro = fast and lively

Allegretto = not too fast

Andante = at a walking pace

legato = smoothly

Maestoso = majestically

Moderato = at a moderate speed

Practissimo = lots of Fiddle Time!

Recording credits

Violins: Ros Stephen, Catrin Win Morgan, Marianne Haynes; *Viola*: Felix Tanner; *Cello*: Laura Anstee; *Piano*: David Blackwell, Julian Rowlands; *Drums and percussion*: Andrew Tween; *Accordion*: Pete Rosser; *Guitars*: Kevin Byrne; *Voice*: Lin Marsh, PR, KB *Engineers*: Ken Blair, Michael Taylor, Jeff Spencer, Ros Stephen; *Programmer*: Andrew McKenna